CONTENTS

MANIPULATION AND PERSUASION

Learn how to Influence Human Behavior, Dark Psychology, Hypnosis, Mind Control, and Analyze People

Joseph Sorensen

INTRODUCTION

Imagine you are in a meeting with a serious investor or a really important date with a partner you intend to marry, and you have the ability to tell what they are thinking. How about understanding the personality of a stranger within minutes of the first meeting? That would be great, right?

All of us would like to succeed in life. However, to achieve this, one needs some special skills. Some of these skills are in you, and all you need to do is harness and practice them, for example, the ability to communicate. Others are not an inborn communicator, and you have to learn them to read another person, for instance.

We are born with the ability to pass messages, persuade, manipulate, and influence others. However, we need to understand these skills and their role in our lives in order to reap their benefits. How can one communicate effectively enough to make others do as he or she wishes without having to force them or using violence?

The following chapters will discuss the power and role of communication in life, the different methods and principles of manipulation and ways of detecting a manipulative attack. Additionally, there is a whole chapter dedicated to ways and tools you can use to read people and understand their personality correctly.

There are plenty of books on this subject on the market; thanks again for choosing this one! Every effort was made to ensure it is full of as much useful information as possible. Please enjoy!

COMMUNICATION TECHNIQUES

Communication is one of the essential parts of human life. It is the most effective tool for passing a message. The way people communicate is very crucial because it determines whether he/she will be understood or misunderstood. The skills one uses to communicate are incredibly necessary for human relations. Interestingly, most people are not entirely conscious of how they communicate. There is a very thin line between conscious and subconscious communication. When we use communication consciously, it is possible to influence people to do what we want even without them realizing it.

On the other hand, it is possible for a person to communicate without being consciously aware of his/her intention. In fact, some people communicate for the sake of communication (talking for the sake of talking). Either way, the message is delivered. Often, we look at communication as the skill of passing information and data verbally, using words. Most of us concentrate on language, that is, the use of words to pass a message. However, in reality, we pass messages in multiple ways, even without realizing it.

. . .

Communication techniques can be used positively or negatively. For instance, a parent may use communication skills with his/her children to control their behaviors. He/she will do this using a technique that will not make the child feel manipulated. So long as the parent is getting positive results from the kid, then that communication is good. However, if a person used these skills to make another fall in love with them without the intention of returning the feelings, then it would be selfish.

Communication skills can be used to pass messages to anyone – from the oldest and wisest person to the youngest and most innocent. The best communication skills enable a person to communicate with different types of people effectively. Better still, good communication skills will help you to influence people in the right direction. People who use communication skills to make others behave in the way they want often defend their actions by saying that they actually want the best for them. For instance, a therapist who is helping a person to get over a drug addiction will use certain communication skills to reach the victim. To some extent, these skills will involve manipulation. However, the therapist has good intentions, and the drug addict will definitely benefit.

On the other hand, some people will use communication skills to control others but cannot point out the benefits that will accrue to the victim. Even when a person is using the communication skills to help another, a crucial question about ethics arises. Why does this person assume that he/she knows what is best for the other, without consulting him/her? There are cases where a person is actually justified to influence another through communication. For instance, if a parent finds out that his/her child is in the wrong gang, he/she has a right and a valid reason to use persuasive communication techniques (to some extent, manipulative ones) to influence the child.

. . .

There are other cases where we might not be justified to use communication skills to influence another without his/her knowledge. True, one can argue that he/she intended to protect the person in question from making a mistake. But, is it okay to prevent people from making mistakes? Is it possible to prevent someone from ever making mistakes? Probably not. Why? Most lessons are learned through experience, which involves mistakes. If we use communication to control others without their consent, is it possible to do it with true respect for the other? Is it okay to intentionally manipulate a person, thus making him/her take the position of a weaker person? If you make someone do what you want, even though they would not do it under normal circumstances, do you think he/she will trust you after realizing what you did?

These are some of the questions everyone should consider before making a conscious choice of influencing people, using whichever skills. What will you do if someone calls you out as a manipulator? Perhaps, the more you hide our intentions toward a person, the higher your chances of breaking that trust.

What we need to clarify is the point at which communication turns into manipulation. When do the storytelling techniques and rhetorical devices used in communication turn from being simply genuine communication tools to those used by manipulators, hypnotists, and psychopaths?

Communication skills should be respectful and honest, which is applicable without hidden intentions. Preferably, we should stick to communication skills that do not waken specific responses or emotions. Our intention should be to steer the other person toward independent and conscious decisions, regardless of the different viewpoints.

The Magic in Communication

Communication is a very powerful and magical tool. It is one of the powers in the world that is common, but very few people understand and acknowledge its power. Communication is probably the only tool that is used by everyone, either knowingly or unknowingly. All the stories we know, our history, myths, pasts, and future predictions are shared through communication. From these stories and myths, we have learned that magic has existed for a long time, and people have used it for both good and evil.

Think of communication as real magic. It can be used for benevolent purposes where we improve the lives of others or for selfish and malicious intentions. On the bright side, communication can be used to communicate feelings or actions of love, hope, and even affection. This is the tool that allows us to share stories and understand one another. At its very worst, this communication is the tool used by malicious and manipulative people to compel and abuse others. When communication is used negatively, it can facilitate injustice, fuel the idea that hate is good, and in the worst-case scenario, incite violence.

Communication, just like magic, appears in many forms. The simple act of imagining something and passing that idea to someone else is magical. Good communication creates shared minds. And by understanding the way a brain works, we are better positioned to communicate efficiently. In fact, the first thing that will facilitate your ability to persuade and manipulate others is effective communication. You need to understand the signs to look out for, the variances between what a person says and does, and the best way to turn a situation to your benefit.

If one knows how to communicate effectively, he/she will have the upper hand over others. One needs to learn how to communicate right using words, emotions, and actions. Communication ensures that we have a shared understanding; therefore, if you understand yourself, it is easy to understand others. Understanding is very important in life because it helps us to determine the best ways of handling different situations.

Communication, manipulation, persuasion, influence, and the ability to read people correctly are connected. However, all of them depend on communication.

HOW TO IMPROVE YOUR MANIPULATION SKILLS

Manipulation is real and happens more often than you could imagine. As such, it is important to understand the art of manipulation and persuasion. You will, once in a while, find yourself in a situation where you need some special techniques to get people to do what you want. Manipulation is such an interesting topic that science has a whole segment dedicated to it. In the 1980s, Dr. Robert Cialdini, the regents' Professor Emeritus of Psychology and Marketing at Arizona State University, did a study on manipulation and persuasion. He compiled a book entitled *Influence: The Psychology of Persuasion*. Manipulation has attracted high levels of attention over the years as more people look for ways either to influence others or avoid manipulation.

Here is the good news; manipulation does not involve arcane art and dark magical powers, and that is also the sad news. See, manipulation is an art that everyone can learn, so long as he/she is determined enough. That means, there is no way of ensuring that only people with good intentions use manipulation techniques.

The first thing to note, Manipulation is very subtle, meaning, the victim is not supposed to realize that the manipulator is controlling him/her. Secondly, manipulation is not about *making* a person do what you want him to do. Rather, it is about getting him to do what you want. This will require you to know yourself and your target.

Thirdly, manipulation is a process, gradual and, in some cases, time-consuming. It is, therefore, important to assess your goals. Are they worth the wait? The factors affecting the time required to get a target to do what you want is dependent of several things, such as the prowess of the manipulator, the exposure between the manipulator and the victim, the techniques used, and other personal factors. This means it will be easier to manipulate someone you spend a lot of time with more than the one you spend little time with.

Finally, manipulation involves force. Although there is no physical force, a person using manipulative techniques will have to push his/her way into the mind of the victim, gently but surely. That force can have a greater impact than physical force.

Technically, there are two types of manipulation — the conscious one and the unconscious one. All of us have engages in the unconscious form of manipulation at one point or the other. In fact, everyone has fallen victim of manipulation at one point or the other. Believe it or not, we meet manipulators every day. When and how, you might ask.

At one moment, a friend might have asked you how you are doing, and you said 'I am fine,' knowing very well that you are not. Your only intention was to divert the attention of that friend by making him/her believe that everything is fine. Well, well, well, that is manipulation. When going for that interview, you actually acted and dressed differently to impress the interviewer. That is a form of manipulation. Even when you lie to your child to make them eat vegetables, you are manipulating them.

If manipulation is so common, then why is it assumed to be wrong? Why do we feel that the word manipulation represents a negative thing? People have, for a long time, thought that manipulation is only used to achieve negative goals. There is no denying that some people actually use manipulation for selfish gains. For instance, you probably know someone who can use manipulation skills to con others. Maybe there is that person you know who gave away a good amount of money courtesy of a manipulative person. Some salespersons will use manipulation techniques to get you to make a purchase, even if they know that the product they are selling is not worthy.

However, that does not mean that everyone uses manipulation skills for selfish benefits. That psychotherapist who uses manipulation to help patients is actually helping them. That parent who is making his/her children eat vegetables using manipulative techniques is doing it for the sake of the children and their health. The bottom line is for you to ask yourself if your intentions are good or bad. Why do you want to get people to do what you want them to do? Who will benefit from the results? Would you want someone to manipulate you the same way? What is the end result?

Because the term manipulation has been used in a negative light for so long, it is better to think of it as persuasion. You want to learn how to persuade people. Manipulation should not be felt or seen. Therefore, you will have to make that person feel like he/she has been making the decisions all along. Basically, women are persuaded by wholesomeness while men are more likely to fall for perfectionism. This means that it is easier to make a man do what you want through things associated with his mastery and ego. Praise a man and massage his ego, and he will do pretty much anything to keep that going. Again, displaying a sense of uncertainty on whether a man can achieve a particular thing will make him try to prove his abilities.

With women, wholesomeness is key. There are many aspects of life which a woman is supposed to balance — family, career, and social life, to name a few. For her, any imbalance will create a burning desire to level things out. Therefore, if you point out an imperfect area in her life, the woman will look for ways to improve it. Certainly, we all need some degree of balance, focus, and sacrifice. However, men tend to lean on perfectionism while women focus on life balance.

Another aspect of human life that affects persuasion and should never be ignored is known as liking and loving tendency. It is an undeniable cognitive bias and a law. A basic example is if Osama Bin Laden said that 5+5 is 10 and Michael Jackson said that 5+5=11. The fact is, Osama is right, and Michael is wrong. However, people would believe Michael (even though he is wrong) and dismiss Osama, even if he is evidently right. Why? The reason is that we associate Osama with the wrong things and Michael with positive things (association bias). What people associate you with determines the degree of influence you will have on them. It is, therefore, important to care about how you make others feel. Know that people may forget what you said, but they will never forget how you made them feel.

Most people who seek to learn manipulation want to apply it in the short run. However, the most successful manipulation tactics are not short-term. You have to love the long game. Sometimes, it will take longer than expected to make a person trust you enough to share details, which you will use to persuade them. Patience is a virtue, and good things are worth waiting for. Have you ever noticed how the world's best-proclaimed artists had gotten their success through simple art? That is what manipulation feels like to your victim — simple and effortless. This person should not even feel pushed around in the lightest way. And that takes time.

One thing that might hurt your manipulation efforts is not understanding Mother Nature and following her flow. You have to read the signs as they are and know when to step back and to push forward. Just like a stone rolling downhill, do not try to force your way against gravity. When it rains, do you start throwing stones at the clouds, demanding that they stop dropping the water, or do you get an umbrella and a raincoat? Obviously, you get a raincoat, and this is "simple adaptation." In some cases, you will have managed to persuade a person 95 percent, then all of a sudden and seemingly from nowhere, the person takes a step back. What do you do then? If you keep pushing, the person might sense something is wrong. It is best to take a step back and wait. Every storm passes. In the meantime, look for another plan.

In simple terms, manipulation and persuasion should not make you delusional. Learn how to adjust to what it is. How can you detect delusion? First, you can spot it if you are expecting a certain output from the wrong input or if you are doing the right thing but in the wrong way or order, for instance, misidentifying your priorities. So to manipulate a person, you have to know his/her personality type, how he/she responds to a certain environment, and what the personal boundaries are. So, how exactly does one manipulate a person?

In order to manipulate a person successfully, you need to be able to do the following:

1. **Know the true desires of a person**. What makes them tick. Then, you will be able to attune those desires toward the goals you would like to accomplish. That is referred to as reverse engineering. The closer you are to a person, the easier it is to manipulate him/her. The degree to which you manipulate a person successfully is directly proportional to your relationship or rather, the degree of trust between you and him/her. That is why manipulation is more likely to succeed between two romantically involved partners than for people who only relate professionally, such as a boss and a junior employee.

1. **Lead with the reward**. Once you have the mental framework out of the way, there is a way to make the person do what you want him/her: rewards and gifts. All of us love rewards. They keep us motivated. You will have to admit that we go to work for the salary or the reward. Some people do not go to work for the salary, but still, there is a catch — the feeling of achievement and the glory of winning — keeps them ticking. We love the dopamine.

So, how can that particular "thing" benefit the person you are persuading? Now, do not tell the person what you want them to do directly. Studies have revealed that most of us hate being told what to do. In fact, 90 percent of the time, we do not want others to dictate our actions and decisions. So, instead of telling that person what you want them to do, make him/her feel like this decision was theirs, and the benefits are largely theirs and not yours. Let a person own it.

Often, we want to take credit for our achievements. However, in persuasion and manipulation, you want the benefits, not the credit. So, if your victim walks around telling others how that particular idea you gave them was theirs, do not try to clarify the facts. You might end up shedding light on the fact that you manipulated the person. Let the person own whatever makes them feel in charge.

The hard part is making the reward feel befitting to the person. You see, if a person cannot see how a particular thing benefits him/her, chances are, he/she will never do it. Again, your choice of words will affect the perception of the other person. For instance, if you are trying to make a person lose weight, and you say something like, " I think you should go on a diet in order to lose weight" chances are, the person will take on the defense. On the other hand, if you talk about how good diet leads to improved skin complexion, the person might actually try to diet. The indirect correlation between great skin completion and maintaining weight can be used to pass a similar message.

There is a saying that goes, you can take cows to the river to drink water, but you cannot force them to drink. The only time they will drink water is when they are actually thirsty. So, Instead of forcing ideas on people, make them thirsty. Curiosity is the ticket. Make a person curious about a particular topic, and you will have nature working in your favor. Do not disobey the laws of nature; just flow with it.

If you think about life genuinely, you will notice all the things that are a scam, yet we are somehow manipulated into believing them 100 percent. Think about higher education. Somehow, we have been made to believe that the only way to succeed in life is through getting the best and highest degrees. To some extent, that is true, but if you think about it more without bias, there are weaknesses in the system that leaves the student exposed to a lot of harsh realities of life. Yet we are stuck on the idea of 13 years of schooling. It is interesting that the school system even makes you follow the long game where you have to wait for a certain number of years before qualifying to the next level. And sadly, we carry on the same ideas to our children.

If you succeed in manipulating people, do not expose yourself. The news of a manipulator spread really fast, so, if one person finds out about your strategies, make sure others will know about it. And the drastic consequences will include being cut off by people. Factually, you do not want that. Make a conscious note of how you are making the people around you feel, then persuade them, only for the best and not evil.

1. **Understand the manipulation funnel.** This is one of the untold tactics in manipulations. There are four steps in the funnel, namely, trust, attention, value, and pain.

These steps follow a particular sequence. For instance, let us assume you are starting a business by selling something. First, you have to catch the attention of your target market and explain the value of your product. However, it will be hard to explain the quantity of value to people who do not trust you or at least have a rapport with. After all, the rule of 'liking and loving applies' here. That is why companies give free samples in the initiation stages of most products.

You have to identify a way of obeying Mother Nature and the rule of association bias tendency to maintain long-term business success. You also need to build that trust. How? Identify something common between you and your target, for instance, an emotional journey or life experiences. This will make the person feel understood, therefore more likely to open up to you. Another thing that can help you build trust is social proof. If other people openly trust you, chances are, other people will trust you, too. Social proof states that people are more likely to do what everyone else seems to be doing.

Congruence is very vital in the establishment of trust. When building that rapport between you and people, void inconsistencies at all costs, more so in your communications about self. You must match what you say with what you do. Again, your way of thinking should lead to your goals. Actions, words, and thoughts must be aligned to ensure that people feel a good vibe when around you; otherwise, you will come off as shady.

Value is created when people feel that they can get a reward from a particular thing. In fact, people will prefer something that helps them achieve a particular goal while they only contribute a little money, time, and energy. That feeling of value (getting the reward) is what drives people to make decisions, buy certain things, love who they choose, and do what they do.

Once a person establishes value in something, he/she tends to proceed with another cognitive bias referred to as "mental accounting." Basically, we tend to compare the value of two items unconsciously. How much do we trust this product over the other? Is it as worth the money as that competing item? For instance, is the content of this book as good as another book that you have read some time back?

If something appears to have no substitute in our heads and is seemingly rare, we tend to attach more value and trust to it, regardless of the situation. For instance, we are more likely to take the advice of a parent because of the trust, value, and level of cherishing we share with them. Even when there is someone with better advice, we will still settle for parental advice. That is the role of trust in influencing other people.

Trust develops from social proof, associative bias, certainty bias, and the liking and loving tendency.

After reaching your victim with value, trust, and attention, it is time to use pain. By this, we do not mean physical pain such as beating up the person. NO. We mean psychological pain, so subtle that the victim will not know it exists, and yet he/she will look for a solution. For instance, in the example of opening a business mentioned earlier, you can use pain to get people to purchase that product. In fact, discounts and offers follow the technique of pain. When that advertisement says, "Buy this product at half the price for the next five days. It will never be this cheap. Why spend more while you can pay less? We guarantee you quality products for a very low price. We are the most trusted company in the country. Get this product now, so you do not miss the opportunity of getting a quality product at a fair price. This offer lasts for only five days," it means it is appealing to your pain.

The advertiser is reminding you of that unconscious pain or discomfort you feel when purchasing that particular item at a higher price. Then, the same advertiser immediately tells you that there is a solution to your pain. The advertising person reminds you that if this opportunity passes, you will be left struggling. He/she also reminds you that the product is of high quality, and it will help solve your problem.

Remember that the closer you are to a person, the easier it is to manipulate them. Successful manipulation takes time. Every situation is unique and will require you to use different tactics. That means the tactics you use on your parents are not the ones you use on your boss. There are tactics that will work on your work colleague but not on your friend. Let us look at some of the people you want to manipulate and the ways to succeed.

1. Parents

Sometimes, our parents fail to give us what we want – mostly because they are trying to protect us. For instance, if you ask your parent for permission to attend a party at a friend's house on a Wednesday (which is a school day), they will probably say no.

Parents are supposed to love their children unconditionally, and that makes them more susceptible to manipulation. That unconditional love should be your weapon. If your parents have a baseline of support and love to the good child, all you have to do is be the model offspring before making your request. Spend time studying, do not miss curfews, be obedient, and help with the house chores as much as you can. Then, once the parent starts seeing the good person in you, go for the kill.

You will have to make your request as if it is perfectly reasonable. If you sound too serious or too desperate, your parents will take the defense and start using logic. You do not want that. For instance, if you want to go to a concert in the middle of a school week, mention it to your parents as if it is the most ordinary thing.

What you want to avoid is sitting down with your parents and explaining about the concert. This allows them time to analyze the details. Make your request so casual that even the parents fail to see the reason for saying no.

Another trick that works perfectly is asking for the favor while doing some house chores, such as folding the laundry or cleaning the dishes. The intention here is to remind your parent of what a good kid you are. Make a casual mention of how every child is doing it, and the other parents were actually okay with it. DO NOT make it a big deal.

Finally, you may use guilt. Make your parents feel guilty for failing you. For instance, if they do not allow you to go to the concert, say something like, "It is okay, I will just ask my friends to bring me a T-shirt or a CD, at least, so I will not feel so left out." Make them feel as if they are making you miss out on something very important. Do not tell your parents that they are ruining your life. That is a big turn off for them. Just play your cards right, and your parents will come to a conclusion on their own, or rather, they will feel as if the decision was theirs.

1. **Spouses**

We all want to have our partners doing exactly what we would like them to. Who doesn't want to go for that dream holiday or at least have a foot rub now and then at will? At the lowest level, manipulating a significant other does not have to be hard. The most obvious way of getting your spouse to do what you want is to turn them on, then ask for the favor. You should imply that if the spouse does not give you what you want, he/she will not get it on. But if you prefer not to use sex as a weapon, there are other more subtle ways. You could use other techniques, which apply to friends.

Regardless of the approach that you choose to use, make sure you remind your partner how sexy you look. Dress up and look lovely. It will remind the person of how special you are.

1. **Friends**

Manipulating a friend can be more tricky than manipulating a stranger because he/she knows you well enough to call your manipulation a bluff if it is not up to par. However, it is still possible to manipulate a friend and make him/her do whatever you want.

First, you have to butter him/her up. The week before you ask for that favor, be nice, offer help, do small but special things, and mention just how great that person is. The intention here is to be that model friend. But do not go overboard. Otherwise, the friend might sense something cooking.

Secondly, use your emotions. The truth is, your true friends will not allow you to go through hard times on your own. They care for you and would not like to see you upset. You will need to look more upset than you really are sometimes. Other times, you might even fake some tears. That will send your friend over the board, trying to help you in whatever way they can.

Third, remind your friend of what a great friend you have always been to him/her. However, you do not want to make them feel like they are being made to pay for something. Point out the times you sacrificed for that friendship, but do not sound demanding.

Finally, invest in guilt-tripping. You really do not want to play the 'bad friend card,' but you might have to make that person feel guilty. Casually mention the times when that friend let you down. Also, make it sound as if you expected it from them as if it is usual for them to leave you when you really need help. Do not sound too accusatory; that might turn them off.

1. **Teacher/lecturers**

This is one of those categories where you cannot use emotions alone. In fact, you will need professionalism. A bit of emotion and professionalism will work for you. First, you have to be the model student before going in for the kill. For instance, finish your work in time, arrive to class early, and show that you have an understanding of the topic being studied. Be active and engaged.

Secondly, make a mention of how great the teacher is without sucking up. You could just mention how inspiring he/she is and how the subject is interesting. Third, involve some emotions. You could mention how things are hard at home — your parents are fighting, or a loved one has passed on. Chances are, awkward things will make the teacher feel sorry for you and offer to help in any way. In fact, make the story so awkward that the teacher will not want to know more. Wait for that moment when the teacher is completely uncomfortable with your story and makes an offer to give you an extension or allow you to rewrite the paper.

If he/she does not offer, initiate the thought by saying something like "I know you do not normally allow students to retake the paper but... " then let your eyes fill up with mist and look away longingly. For this, you will need to put your acting skills into play. If the teacher is still not buying it, go for the strings of the heart. You could start being hysterical and shedding tears over the 'things going on at home.' Wait until the teacher gets uncomfortable, then he will give in to what you want.

1. **Bosses**

Now, this is a slippery one because a wrong move could get you fired. The best way to get a boss to do or give you what you want is through logic and reasoning. Most managers do not use emotions when handling business, and that is one of the things that makes them good at running those organizations and businesses. If you show up at your boss' desk and start crying because of all the things going on at home, chances are, you will get fired (or be given an unpaid leave to sort your personal issues and get better). So, the best way to deal with a boss is by being firm and logical. Gather concrete reasons for your request, and be ready to defend your stand.

Be the model worker the week before going for your kill. You could work a little late, bring pastries to the office, and keep a bright smile on your face, just because you are 'positive.' When making that request, do it in an offhand-ish way. Make the request sound like it is a 'no big deal' rather than saying something like, "Hello, there is something serious I wanted to talk to you about." This statement will alert the boss that whatever you are about to ask is really important and will require some thorough considerations.

Also, there are certain hours of the day when the boss is likely to give in to your request than others. For instance, if talking to the boss during break or at the end of the day, he/she is likely to give in. Why? Because, during breaks, the boss wants to go out rather than spend time arguing with you. The same applies for evenings. The boss will easily say yes to get past the conversation because he/she wants to go home after a long day at work.

Avoid talking to the boss in the morning when he/she has a lot to do for the day and is worried about numerous things. Also, go for those moments when the boss is relaxed. Remember that bosses are human beings, too, and should not be feared. They, too, have emotions, strengths, and weaknesses.

The ease at which a person falls into your manipulation trap is determined by the impression you have on him/her. In some cases, you will have to be a sweet and charming person while in others, flexible and swift. Either way, you will have to be wise in how you project yourself. Be deceptive if you must.

Use emotions to get what you want. Do your loved ones want to see you sad, crying, or visibly upset? No. Emotions work best with spouses and friends.

In other situations, you might opt to use the waterworks approach, more so in public. Just like a parent is more likely to give in to the demands of a child if he/she throws a tantrum in public, so are you more likely to get what you want from a spouse if you are crying in public. However, it is better to use this technique sparingly.

Small bribes also work quite well. For instance, if you want your girlfriend to accompany you to the baseball game tomorrow, take her out for dinner tonight. Then, this becomes more like an ordinary compromise and less manipulation.

Improve Your Manipulation

Manipulation and persuasion might sound easy and selfish, but they are not. It takes a lot to become a master manipulator. Getting what you want from people is not just a walkover. Whether it is making your spouse to accompany you to an even they hate or tricking your boss into giving you a pay rise or making your parents to give you money for that expensive dress, you will need skills. You will need to learn the techniques and hone your skills. Below are some of the steps you can follow to improve your manipulation technique.

1. *Take an acting class.*

Emotions are the giveaways of most people, and you will gain more if you learn how to manipulate them. The biggest part of manipulation is learning how to master your own emotions and making others receptive to you. That means, in some cases, you will have to appear more worried than you really are, maybe even force some real tears. Other times, you will have to appear more impressed or distressed. Such a skill will require you to take an acting class. It will help you to improve your power of persuasion.

Do not tell other people that you are taking an acting class if the reason is to learn how to manipulate others. They might grow suspicious and start taking a defensive stance and being wary of your tactics.

1. *Join a public speaking class.*

The most common way of communication is verbal. An acting class will help you to master your emotions and effectively convince others to do what you want. But it might not teach you how to put your needs into words effectively. A debate class of public speaking sessions can help you to verbalize your emotions. You will learn how to organize your ideas and present them constructively. Besides, you will learn how to sound more convincing.

1. *Establish similarities*

We tend to feel comfortable and share more when we are around people we have things in common. When it comes to manipulation, you need to make that victim feel comfortable. The basic tactic for establishing similarities is called pacing, where you mirror the body language and intonation patterns of the other person.

. . .

Use a calm and persuasive technique to manipulate people who prefer logic and rationality.

1. *Be charismatic*

Basically, human beings lean toward charming people more than gloomy ones. That is why charismatic people seem to have a natural tendency of getting what they want. If you want to manipulate people successfully, work on your charisma. Be charming to the extent that a simple smile from you lights up the room. Make sure you are the person whom people remember when they think of nice moments. Also, people should know that you are dependable and understanding; therefore, they will open up to you more easily.

Your body language should be approachable, such that people open up to you more. Besides, you should be able to hold a conversation with anyone, be it a nine-year-old kid or a 75-year-old retiree. Some of the ways you can be charismatic include:

1. Make people feel special. You can do this by making and maintaining eye contact during conversations, asking them about their interests and feelings, and showing genuine care. Show the person that you really want to know these details about him/her, even if you do not care.

1. Show confidence. Charismatic people tend to display high self-esteem. People tend to follow those who are confident and seem sure of their words. If you have faith in yourself, people will believe you. However, if you are unsure of what

you are talking about, most people will hardly listen to you twice. Whatever you do or say, be it true or false, apply confidence. If possible, be glib when talking to your targets.

1. *Learn from the masters.*

The easiest way to learn is by observing experts. If you have a friend, relative, or boss who is a master manipulator, it is time to study them. What do they say? How do they pose? What is their winning trick? How do they talk-manipulate words? Take notes of what these people do to make an analysis. This will give you an inner view of the tools used by manipulators. Note, however, that you might end up getting tricked by the manipulator as you watch him/her.

You are more likely to gather information about manipulators by watching one. Furthermore, if you are committed to understanding how manipulators get their way, studying the experts is a sure way.

1. *Read people.*

To be a successful manipulator, you must learn how to read different people. If you understand what a person is going through, it will be easier to manipulate him/her. It is also easier to follow the natural flow of your victim if you understand him/her.

Every person has a different psychological and emotional setup; therefore, you cannot use the same manipulation technique on everyone. Before plotting a manipulation plan and scheme, take time to understand the target. What makes him/her tick? What is the high and low? What are the strengths and weaknesses? What tools can you use to bend them?

Below are some of the things you are likely to observe when reading people.

1. A large number of people are emotional, meaning, they are highly susceptible to emotional responses. Such people tend to cry at movies or get smitten by cute puppies. Also, these people have strong empathy and sympathy powers. To make these people bend to your will, play with their emotions. Share a sad story so that they can feel sorry for you and offer to help.

1. Another group of people is highly susceptible to guilt. They have a strong guilt reflex. This often happens to those who were raised in strict households and restrictive society. If a person was punished for every mistake, chances are, he/she will walk through life feeling guilty for everything they do and fail to do. With such people, all you have to do is play the guilt string. Make them feel guilty for failing to help you, so they would do it. Make them feel guilty for doing a thing, so they would stop.

1. Then, there is the rational team or a group of people who only follow the logic. If your target always has a level head, follows the logic, reads the news every day, knows the facts, and likes evidence before getting into anything, you will have to use the calm, persuasive powers instead of emotions.

Techniques of Manipulations

There are a variety of manipulation techniques you can use. However, some are more successful than others. Below are some of the techniques you can use

1. **Door in the face.** Basically, this technique involves making an unreasonable request, then following it up with one that seems more reasonable. This technique has been tested over the years and is an almost sure bet. Simply, make an outrageous request, wait for the person to reject it, then make a reasonable one. Technically, the second request will sound more appealing to the victim compared to the first one, and in fact, he/she will not have much time to think about other options.

For instance, ask a person for 100 dollars, and if he/she says no, ask for 10 dollars only. That will sound like a very reasonable option, and the person will become more receptive.

1. **Foot in the door.** This technique is the opposite of the door in the face technique, where you ask for a favor from a person, and if they accept, you ask for a bigger favor. The trick is to sound as reasonable and logical as possible. For instance, "Mum, can you please assist me with 50 dollars to buy a new book?" If she says yes, add "Or, can you please make it 80 so that I can also get some revision materials?"
2. **Ask for the unusual then follow it with the usual.** This technique is intended to throw the victim off-balance, more like the foot in the door technique. In most cases, people will subconsciously notice the kind of favors you tend to ask for and have some prepared responses. Again there are normal tasks which people know how to avoid, such as giving people rides home, giving financial support, or even helping with homework. Minds get conditioned to avoid these tasks.

To throw someone off balance, you could ask them to get you some medicine over lunch hour because your foot is aching, then ask them to give you a ride home. The first request is not a common day-to-day occurrence. Therefore, it throws your target off balance.

1. **Relief after fear.** Nobody likes to be afraid, and everyone appreciates the relief of finding that their worries were false or at least they have been solved. Fear has been used over the years to get people to give in. You, too, can use this emotion to manipulate people. Basically, the feeling of relief makes one so happy that he/she will hardly say no. For instance, you can tell your boyfriend, "You know, the other day I almost got mugged. I was walking in the street, and some guys were following me. I do not know what was on their mind. I had to dive into the first pub I saw. Who knows what would have happened if they had caught me. I am really lucky. Which reminds me, can I borrow your car this weekend? I do not want to walk on my own, and I also do not want to bother you by making you drive me around."

2. **Make your target to feel guilty.** This is an excellent way of making a person to give you what you want. This technique works best for people who are already prone to guilt. Then make the person feel like he/she is bad regardless of how ridiculous your request sounds. For instance, if your parents are already feeling guilty for their weaknesses in raising you, make them feel like they are ruining your life more by failing to permit you to attend that party. If it is your friend, pull the guilt string by reminding him/her of all the times you have been there for him/her, yet he/she is failing you. If you want your boyfriend or girlfriend to feel guilty for not doing that favor, just say, "It's okay, I expected that." This will make him/her like he/she has been letting you down for long, and it is time to make up for it.

3. **Play the victim.** As unusual as it may sound, playing the victim has made many people win cases. It is a position we

hate to put yourself in, but being the victim might actually get that target to give in to your plan. However, do not overdo it. As much as it is a great technique, one should only use it sparingly. This is because most people will not like to help you every time just because you are the helpless victim.

4. **First, you have to act like the most amazing, light-hearted, and altruistic person in the world.** Then, make the target believe that all the evil in the world has befallen you, and you just cannot understand why. You could spice it up by saying, "I just cannot figure out what I keep doing wrong." You have to sound genuinely baffled by why your life is not working out as you had hoped. If the person has turned your request down, Say, "It is okay; I am used t this." That will trigger guilt and make the person want to help you.

If a friend has refused to give you a ride home, be pathetic and say, "It's okay; I will walk. It is even helpful for me as exercise."

1. **Bribery.** Yes, it is wrong, but we all have to admit it; bribery can be useful in desperate situations. In this case, we are not necessarily talking about bribing with money only. You will have to be more creative, depending on who your victim is. What does that person want? Try giving it to him/her and get your favor in return. For instance, if your friend has a crush on the cute boy/girl in school, tell him/her that you will get the phone number if he/she does your homework. However, do not make it that obvious.

2. **Apply logic.** Remember, there are people you cannot just manipulate with emotions and a few simple reasons. Some people use a lot of logic before making any decisions. So, you will need logic and rationalism. Be armed with all the reasons, result-oriented ones, for why you want a certain thing done in that particular way. Be ready to defend your answer—patiently. Talk calmly and confidently, be rational,

and keep your emotions out of it. Again, keep your emotions out of it.

Act like whatever you want is the most logical thing. Act as if you have analyzed every option and come up with all the facts. Make the person look irrational for not seeing things as you do.

1. **Do not break character.** Repeat this loudly — do NOT break character. Most of us will budge under the weight of accusation, more so if it is true. However, as a manipulator, you should never admit to using these tactics. If a friend or co-worker calls you out for being manipulative, deny that. Act shocked and say something like, "What? I cannot believe you can think of me that way." Do it in a way that makes the person feel guilty.

You could even accuse him/her of being jealous for a certain thing, gently. The people listening to your accuser will feel sorry for you. If you ever admit to using manipulative techniques, it will immediately become hard for you to ever use those techniques again on the same people. You will be surprised to see how fast such news spreads. Everyone will know about what you have been up to and be on the lookout.

14 TIPS TO UNDERSTAND MANIPULATION ATTACKS

Everyone has met a toxic person at least once in their life. There are many types of toxic people in the world, and if you have not encountered such a person, you will meet one someday. Psychopaths, malignant narcissists, and people with antisocial behavioral traits often engage in maladaptive behaviors in relationships. In most cases, they end up exploiting, demeaning, and hurting others, knowingly or unknowingly. Consequently, they lose people close to them.

Manipulative people apply a variety of diversionary tactics to distort the reality of their victims and deflect responsibility. Sometimes, people who are not narcissist use these tactics. However, the narcissists use these manipulation tools to an excessive extent while trying to avoid responsibilities and accountability. If you want to know the twenty most used tactics of manipulation, keep reading because they are listed and explained in the simplest language.

Gaslighting

This is a manipulation technique that can be described in a number of short sentences. They include, "That did not happen" "Are you crazy?" "You imagined it." Gaslighting is one of the most common and insidious tactics of manipulation. It works through distorting or eroding your sense of reality. Gradually, gaslighting eats away at one's ability to trust his/her instinct and judgment. Inevitably, anyone who is a victim of gaslighting loses the power to call out the abuser because he/she is unsure of his/her judgment.

When a manipulative and toxic person constantly gaslights you, cognitive dissonance arises within you. In an attempt to reconcile that gap, you will most probably gaslight yourself. That is when you find yourself doubting your judgments. In the process, you allow the victimizer to hurt you more. The conflict between 'Is this person right?' and 'can I trust myself?' become so intense that you no longer know what to believe. A manipulator will convince you that your judgments are wrong. In fact, you will start feeling dysfunctional.

The best way to handle gaslighting and resist or avoid it is through self-grounding. This means that you have to trust yours on reality. Write down the facts if you must. For instance, if you notice that someone has the habit of making promises, then denying them, write the promise down. Mark the dates. Note down the things that happened or get someone else involved so that he/she can remind you or be your proof. Have a validating community — it has the power to redirect you from a distorted reality and back to your inner guide.

Projection

This is the habit of denying one's shortcomings and always blaming others. We all sometimes project, especially when we do not want to face the consequences of our actions. It is a defense mechanism we learn from a very tender age. However, projection becomes a problem when it is chronic. If one does not want to accept a mistake or own responsibility at all times, then that is dangerous. Basically, manipulators will not project their good deeds on another person, but they will want to push the bad things away from their circle. If one can accept the good, he/she should also embrace the bad.

· · ·

The difference between how normal people and narcissists use projection is that the latter group are psychologically abusive. Instead of owning one's weaknesses, the manipulative psychopaths and malignant narcissists opt to throw their own imperfections, flaws, and wrongdoings to their unsuspecting victims. The saddest part is that they do it in a painful and excessively cruel manner, making the victim feel intimidated or like less of a person.

Instead of admitting that self-improvement is in order, the manipulative people would rather put the blame on others, and make them feel the shame. For instance, a person who engages in pathological lying can accuse others of fibbing. A needy person may accuse his/her partner of being clingy in an attempt to make others see this person as the dependent one. A rude employee will call their boss selfish or ineffective to avoid the truth about their failures and lack of productivity.

Majority of narcissistic abusers love to play the blame game, and their objective is to win while you lose. If they lose, blame-gamers will shift the blame of everything that is wrong to you and the world. This way, you get to babysit their selfish and fragile ego. On the other hand, you drown in the sea of self-doubt and self-blame.

The solution to chronic projection is not to allow these toxic people to blame you for their weaknesses. Do not allow yourself to show empathy or compassion for someone who is projecting on you. They do not deserve it. If you show a manipulative people that you actually feel for them, chances are, they will keep exploiting you. Stand up for yourself and refuse to be responsible for other people's mistake.

Narcissists are on the furthest end of the human behavior spectrum and have no desire to acknowledge or even change their behaviors. It is very important to cut ties with people who lack self-insight and desire for change. Stay away from manipulative and toxic people in order to validate your own identity and rediscover your reality. There is no good enough reason for you to exist in a cesspool of dysfunction created by someone else.

Senseless Conversations

Mind manipulative people know how to evade conversations that might expose them. They do not want to share too much important information with others. Therefore, they will do anything to avoid tough conversations. So if you thought there is a chance of having a thoughtful conversation with a mind manipulative person, here is a surprise for you — be prepared for one of the most thoughtless and mindless conversations.

Malignant psychopaths, sociopaths, and narcissists use word salad, jargons, circular conversations, projection, gaslighting, and hominem arguments to disorient you and drive the conversation off the track. If you challenge or disagree with their opinion, be ready for an epic, senseless argument. They do this to confuse, frustrate, and discredit you, driving you away from the real problem and making you feel guilty for initiating the conversation. When arguing with a manipulator, you will feel like it is wrong to have your thoughts and feelings. You will be required to agree with their opinion at every turn; failure to do so will create a problem.

Spend five minutes arguing with a narcissist, and you will even find yourself wondering what the conversation was really about. You could even correct them about facts like the sky is red or the world is flat, and they will attack everyone in your circle, friends, relatives, career choices, food preferences, political affiliation, et cetera. In the end, you will not know what the talk was about. That is because pointing out the facts picks on their false beliefs, and that hurts their narcissistic ego.

. . .

Point to note: Narcissists, psychopaths, and other manipulative people do not hold a conversation with you, rather, they essentially argue with themselves and make you unwarily become privy to their excessive and draining monologue. Most manipulative people live for the drama and thrive off it. Every time you try to provide a point that beats their crazy assertions, you are simply feeding their supply. Brace yourself for more drama.

Do not fall for the monologue traps of manipulators. Do not feed their selfish supply. Remind yourself that their weak behavior is their problem and has nothing to do with you. Stop the conversation as soon as the manipulator starts to get crappy. Cut all interactions once you realize that the person is just moving in circles and avoiding the real facts. Use your precious energy to do other constructive things.

Blanket Statements

This is a situation where a person used one statement to generalize everything. Although most manipulators are intellectual masterminds and professional skimmers, some of them are mentally lazy. Instead of taking the time to analyze the situation as is, they generalize everything you say and do. Their statements and conclusions do not pay homage to the different nuances in your arguments.

Manipulators will avoid taking into account the multiple perspectives of your situations because they might find that you were right or justified. Some will go to the extreme of putting a label on you all together to avoid considering your perspective. For instance, a manipulator can label you as a bad mom, so, if you punish your child for something they did wrong, the manipulator will not stop to understand why you did that. Instead, he/she will just call you a bad mom, and that is final.

On the larger scale, blanket statements and generalities are used to invalidate the experiences that do not fit in certain assumptions, stereotypes, and schemas. Furthermore, they are used to maintain a predetermined status quo. Sadly, these generalizations can obscure justice in some cases. For instance, if a person reports a rape case when the accused rapist is a well-liked figure, generality will remind us that there are many false rape cases raised against innocent people. Consequently, the actions of a group of people become labeled as the way of many, and the facts of the case itself get ignored.

Generalization also occurs a lot in abusive relationships where, if a person complains that the behavior of the manipulator is unacceptable, he/she will take the defense and call the accuser "always oversensitive" or "never satisfied." By making such statements, the manipulator avoids sorting out the real issue and at the same time, makes the victim feel like a bad person, all the time. It is possible that the accuser is oversensitive at times, but again, maybe the partner is manipulative and uses generalizations.

The best way to deal with generalities is by holding on to your truth. Make sure that the person using generalities listens to the details of each case scenario. Remember that manipulators who use blanket statements tend to think in black and white, leaving no room for colors and greys. That is an insensitive and illogical way of thinking. Just because someone can use generalities, it does not mean that he/she has experienced the full wealth of experience. It only displays an overinflated sense of self and the limitedness or lack of experience.

Deliberate Misinterpretation of Feelings, Words, and Thoughts

Manipulators play around with the minds of their victims. In fact, they will mess with your thoughts, feelings, and words so much that you will start to feel absurd. Your differing opinions, experiences, and legitimate emotions get translated as evidence of your irrationality and character flaws. A narcissist will weave a tall tale to simply reframe what you said and make it sound like the most senseless and illogical thing.

In fact, your thoughts and experiences will appear heinous in the presence of a narcissist. For instance, if you are telling a narcissistic friend that the way they talk is not good, they might say, "Oh, now you want to behave like the perfect one?" "Or, are you implying that I am a bad person?' All you did was express your feeling in a genuine way, and now, it turns into a battle. Deliberate misinterpretation allows one to invalidate your rights to have feelings, thoughts, opinions, and emotions. You should not try to talk about inappropriate behavior practiced by the manipulator, and if you do, they will make you feel guilty. Deliberate misinterpretation also prevents one from setting a boundary.

This deliberate misinterpretation is, in some cases, what people mistake as "mind-reading." This cognitive distortion is used by toxic people who presume that they know what you are feeling and thinking; therefore, they jump to conclusions based on assumptions and personal triggers. Instead of stepping back and evaluating the situation, the manipulators act according to their baseless delusions and fallacies. To make matters worse, these people are unapologetic about the harm they cause after making wrong assumptions.

Manipulators put words in your mouth and portray you as having an outlandish viewpoint which you did not possess at first. They will accuse you of thinking of them as manipulators even before you have the chance to call them out. That is a form of pre-emptive self-defense

If you realize that someone is putting words in your mouth, simply say, "I did not say that" and walk away. Trying to argue your case in such a situation will only earn you a quarrel and long disagreement that will have no sensible conclusion. It can also help if you put boundaries for people who use this technique to manipulate you.

Remember that so long as a person can shift the blame to you, he/she already has the chance to make you feel miserable because every time you give valid feedback, this manipulator will find a way to invalidate it.

Moving the Goalposts and Nit-Picking

Constructive criticism is helpful and useful. On the other hand, destructive criticism is selfish. The main difference between constructive and destructive criticism is personal attacks and irrational standards/demands. Most of the people who engage in destructive criticism do not want to help. Instead, they just want to make you feel bad by nit-picking every mistake and wrong turn you make. They will use a scapegoat and pull you down in all ways. Sociopaths and abusive narcissists are known for nit-picking. They also employ another fallacy called moving the goalposts. Technically, you will never be good enough for such people regardless of your actions. As soon as you reach a target they set, these manipulators add something new to show you that you are incompetent. You will provide all the proof supporting your argument, and still, they will ask for more.

If you already have a successful career, a manipulative narcissist will start to explain to you why you are not a multi-billionaire yet. Interestingly, this person does not even have the qualifications you have. Are you independent? Now, it is time to prove that you are never needy or cling. The goals set by these people will always change, and they might not even be related to each other. A manipulator will be perpetually dissatisfied with you, and you will feel lacking you if their validation matters a lot in your life.

These people will instill in you a sense of complete worthiness and 'being never enough' by raising the standards higher and higher every time. In some cases, these manipulators will change the goalposts completely. In fact, they will hyper-focus on the one thing you did wrong and distract you from your strength. Gradually, you, too, will focus on your flaws and weaknesses, nit-picking on those irrelevant facts. The manipulative person will make to concentrate on the next thing he/she will point out and get you obsessing about what you did not achieve. You will bend over backward until it hurts, and still, the manipulator will not change the way he/she treats you.

The solution is not to get sucked into the endless game of nit-picking and changing goals. That will only distract you from your real purpose. If a person chooses to keep repeating the same small matter over and over, it is not your problem. The person is just trying to justify why he/she is unsatisfied with your work. Their real intention is just to make you feel the need to keep proofing yourself to them. And so long as you feel this way, they have a chance to use you. Know that you are good enough, and no one can change that. If a person does not like the way you do things and keeps criticizing you destructively, it is time to set boundaries.

Changing the Subject

This is a technique used to divert attention. It can also be called the 'what about me syndrome.' Basically, you will tell a manipulator something, and he/she will make it about himself/herself. It works in a similar way as the senseless conversation technique. The person will destruct you from the real problem by making the talk about him/herself. For instance, you might question a partner about their lack of accountability, and he/she will start talking about the tough childhood, the bad parents, the tough job, et cetera. In the end, you will not solve anything.

To avoid this technique, you must learn how to stay on topic and not get derailed. If someone tries to pull a switcheroo on you, apply what is called the broken record. Keep talking about the real topic even when the person is pushing you to other subtopics. Make sure that you are heard. If the person is too stubborn, simply walk away and initiate the conversation later. If he/she still tries to derail you, be courageous enough to call him/her out.

·   ·   ·

Note that in order to solve any issue, being specific is needed. By allowing people to keep taking you away from the real conversation, you are creating room for a list of unresolved matters. Stay focused, and make sure that the other person knows and acknowledges the conversation. If you have tried engaging a person in the real conversation and he/she still seems uninterested, disengage, and spend your energy elsewhere. You do not have to hold conversations with manipulative people who have the mental age of a toddler.

Name-Calling

As childish as it may sound, this is their selfish supply. The name-calling technique is used by many people. We have heard politicians calling each other names on public podiums, parents insulting each other in divorce courts, Kids verbally harassing each other in backyards, and other similar instances. Narcissists have the tendency of blowing up anything that does not fit in their description. If they perceive anything as a threat, that is a good enough reason for them to destroy it. In their world, manipulative people are always right, and anyone who states otherwise deserves to be put down.

At the lowest and most intimidating opportunities, the manipulators resort to narcissistic rage, especially the name-calling. Whenever a narcissist lacks a way of micromanaging your emotions and opinions, he/she uses insults you as the easiest way of putting you down. If you lack wit, chances are, the names will make you feel worthless and socially valueless.

Name-calling is often used to insult your intelligence, behavior, and appearance, criticize your insights, opinions, and beliefs, and destroy your right to be a separate person altogether. A topic you had done thorough research on suddenly becomes an idiotic or silly opinion in the hands of a manipulator who cannot make a sensible and convincing rebuttal. Rather than countering your argument respectfully, the manipulators will attack you as a person.

You must end any conversations that turn into name-calling. Such talks will only hurt your ego. People who use name-calling to attack you lack a better method of defending their opinion, and if you know better, you should not stoop that low.

Destructive Conditioning

Manipulators and other toxic people want you in a position where they can harm you. As such, they will look for ways to make you feel miserable and vulnerable. One way to make you a victim is destructive conditioning. The manipulator will condition you to see everything in a negative light. They will associate your talents, strengths, and happy memories with disrespect, abuse, and frustrations. They do this by showing you that they, too, once had the same experiences that turned out wrong. You can tell a manipulative person about a camping trip that was fun and mention that one camper was bitten by a snake — he/she will focus on the snake section of the story, ignoring all the other good things.

When these toxic people force you to pay attention to the negative bit, they are looking for a way to get the attention back to themselves. The spotlight has to be on them only. This is because most narcissists are pathologically envious. They do not want anything between you and them, including your happiness. A bright moment in your life reminds them of their boring one.

To avoid this, first, understand and acknowledge that you do not need validation from toxic people. They do not care about you or your happiness. And if you do not need their negativity in your life, why don't you just leave them? The destructive condition can keep you short of your dreams and feeling as if walking on eggshells. Do you really want that kind of life?

Aggressive and Hurtful Jokes

Hopefully, by now, you have realized that manipulative narcissists and psychopaths are only looking for ways to keep you in their control box. They make you vulnerable enough to be manipulated. One way to intimidate you is by making aggressive jabs at you then claiming it was a joke. They will make senseless and malicious jokes about you then if you complain, they would say you are too sensitive or that your sense of humor is lacking. Here is the thing; if a 'joke' has hurt you, it is not funny and could be a disguise.

A person who lacks a way of attacking you directly will make a harsh remark and still maintain a cool demeanor. A toxic person gains pleasure from hurting you and getting away with it. The best way to deal with such a person is to call them out. Stand up for yourself, and make it clear that you will not tolerate such behavior. The manipulator will try to gaslight you, but make sure that your facts are right.

Covert and Overt Threats

Toxic people and narcissists do not like anyone who threatens their overbearing sense of entitlement. They do not want you to challenge their sense of superiority. So, instead of tackling disagreements maturely or agreeing to disagree, manipulators will set out to divert your attention from the facts by instilling fear in you through threats.

If someone is pulling this tactic on you, be wary of them. You might be dealing with a dangerous psychopath who might actually solidify the threats. Take every threat as a red flag, and get away from such manipulators. They are not worth your time.

Stalking and Smear Campaigns

Manipulative and toxic people will always try to control you. If they cannot achieve this goal, these manipulators start to attack you indirectly. The toxic people label you as a bad person while acting like the martyrs. A lot of manipulative people will initiate a smear campaign with the intention of sabotaging your reputation and slandering your name. A smear campaign is used to ensure that a person has no team to support them if they decide to walk away from the manipulator.

. . .

Abusive manipulators also tend to stalk their victims and harass them in the name of exposing the truth. Some crazy ones will go to the extent of threatening the loved ones of their victims. All this is meant to cover the truth about their behavior.

The best way to handle such people is by sticking to the facts and staying mindful of your reactions. Any display of fear or being shaken is taken as a sign of weakness, and the manipulator will use that more. Document every harassment, stalking, or cyberbullying incidences. If you are facing manipulative ex-partner, use a lawyer. Do not try to fight them back or engage in the smear campaigns. Your integrity and character will speak for itself.

Love Bombing and Devaluation

Narcissists and toxic people ensure that you are invested enough and sufficiently hooked to them. This way, it becomes easy for you to accept their friendship and keep their company. Then they start to devalue you to make you small enough for their manipulation. They will call you stupid and make you feel the need to prove otherwise. Narcissistic partners are known to abuse their partners and ex-partners. Once that cycle is in motion, you are done.

The first step to dealing with such people is to slow down interactions. Once you suspect that a person is toxic, take a step back and analyze them. You can tell whether a person is toxic or not by the way they talk about others. Watch out for that. It is not up to you to change them, and it is even safer for you to stop such interactions.

Pre-Emptive Defenses

Have you ever met a person who stresses just how nice he/she is and that you should trust them — immediately? Chances are, that person is not good, and you should be wary. Many manipulative and toxic people tend to overstate their 'kindness and compassion.' They tell you endless stories of how they helped and so and so, making it look like they are the most helpful people on earth. That is a pre-emptive defense and is intended to throw you off balance. If you detect such behavior, it is time to run or stay strategic. Genuine people will rarely insist on telling you about every good thing they ever did for others.

METHODS OF MANIPULATION

Manipulation is everywhere — people use manipulative techniques more often. In fact, the conversation about manipulation has become quite loud. Every day, you will notice someone talking about how another person has been manipulating him/her. You will also notice more people trying to manipulate you, especially now that you have studied the techniques used by most manipulators. The real question is, how one can set boundaries that deter manipulators effectively? How can you set limits in the face of people who are using manipulative techniques to get to you?

First, note that there are many different ways used to manipulate people. Every technique can be customized according to the situation. The impact of manipulation is even greater if the victimizer is a master manipulator. The only sure way of dealing with different forms of manipulation is to understand the methods of manipulation. If you know what to look out for, then you will know when to resist or run. Yes, there are times when you will have to walk away from the manipulator instead of confronting him/her. The following discusses some of the methods used by manipulators and how you can identify and deal with them. Understanding these techniques will also help you to maintain your boundaries. You will also understand why these techniques work on people and how they do. What can one do to defend themselves against them?

First, let us assess why people want to manipulate other people. In a short explanation, we can say that manipulators and the manipulated are like two sides of the same coin. They are all looking for a response from others. We think that the manipulators are the only ones who have the need to control others. However, that is not true. Even the manipulated people have this urge. However, this need shows in different ways. The manipulator wants to get his/her needs met while the manipulated allows the victimizer to use them in order to fill the need to be needed, loved, or cared for. For instance, when a boyfriend gives in to the manipulative desires of his girlfriend, he is trying to avoid being seen as a bad boyfriend. And so long as the girlfriend thinks that this boyfriend is good, then he is in control, somehow.

Both the manipulators and the manipulated are looking for a way to feel safe — like they are worthy or are making a contribution to the world. The person being manipulated is trying to offer services to others to please others in exchange for something like love, food, or being noticed. On the other hand, the manipulator is getting an almost similar sense of value recognition, admiration, or power, but he/she is using control. Manipulators feel that if they can make you do things you would not normally do, then they have control over you. So long as they have this power, they feel important. In some cases, they feel like you care about them, and that is why some of the manipulators use the phrases "If you care about me, then you must do this and that."

Honestly, it would be really nice just to tell everyone to stop being manipulative. However, it is not actually possible or even realistic. Manipulators do not want to be discovered, so they do everything secretly. Technically, in life, we are not in a position to manifest our ideas in the reality of someone else, but we can adjust our own. We cannot stop other people from doing whatever they want, but we are in control of how we react to them. You can try changing people, but that does not really work. The only time a person change is when he/she chooses to. To deal with manipulators and other negative energies in our life, we need to own that power. Own your power and change the vibration so that a manipulator cannot use you.

As you read through these methods of manipulation, you might identify that some people in your life are actually using them. Do not start a confrontation immediately; instead, take your time to understand where their unethical need is coming from. Note that these techniques are about you, not the other person (manipulators), and if you want to look for ways to punish the manipulator, you cannot find them here.

Gaslighting

This method of manipulation has been existent for centuries and has been used by millions of manipulators successfully. Basically, gaslighting is intended to make you doubt yourself. For instance, a manipulative partner can convince you that your boundaries are outrageous or ridiculous. So, when that partner does something that bothers you, and you complain about it, he/she will make it look irrelevant. In fact, he/she will reduce it t nothing. You will get offended by something the manipulators do or say, and if you mention it, they will tell you something like, "This is so stupid," "That is so absurd," "Does that even sound sensible to you?" or"That would not even bother me at all." Why is it that you are the only one who seems bothered? You are just overly sensitive. No one is safe from this method because when a manipulator uses it, he/she is looking for a lowered boundary or a loophole, which is a way to control you.

If a manipulator uses this technique on you often, you might start believing that your decisions and boundaries are invalid. Gradually, you will drop them to accommodate this person. Here is the fact; the boundaries you have are not set by anyone else but you. Technically, you are the only person who really understands your life, goals, and limits. Nobody else should get to determine the boundaries you can set. You know what bothers you, and no one else gets to feel pain for you. So, if someone is pinching you constantly and you tell him/her to stop because you are not enjoying it, they should listen to you. However, It is really irritating that this person can tell you something like, "Ohh, you are such a baby. I am not even pinching you hard. It is playful." He/she does not feel your pain, so do not feel intimidated by their words. It is not up to any other person to decide what you should and should not tolerate.

When making your boundaries known, first, understand that those boundaries are yours — not theirs. Again, you have valid reasons to set your boundaries. It is not just a boundary for the sake of boundaries. If someone disrespects your boundaries, call him/her out, confidently, and make them soft. If they dare to question your boundaries, you should be strong enough to fight back. Note that there is a big difference between setting boundaries and controlling other people. Boundaries are about you. They help and protect you, whereas control is about them — choosing and determining who says what and who does what.

So, setting boundaries is not about making people stop living the way they want; rather, it is about making them understand that there are consequences to certain things in your life. For instance, when you set a boundary for how people talk to you, it does not mean that everyone will follow your rules. Neither does it mean that you should make them follow your decisions. It means that you will walk away from anyone who oversteps you without apologies. You get to choose who to engage with and who to walk away from. It is more like saying, "You do not get to mess with things in my house, but if you want to do something like this, go mess your own house." Remember, if someone gaslights you constantly, it is time to walk away from them.

Rage Beasts

This is a technique where the manipulative person gets to be angrier than what the situation called for. The person gets more upset than you. The intention here is to squash your emotions as fast as possible. For instance, you might be talking to someone about something they did, and instead of reasoning with you, this person explodes really loud with rage, and it becomes such drama that you find yourself withdrawing in shock. You will be turned off because that situation did not call for such a reaction, and you just cannot figure out what you said that pushed that person to the edge. And because you would rather avoid drama rather than deal with it, you will yourself to walk away.

Consequently, you do not set boundaries. You do not even stand up for yourself because the person you are going up against is a rage. To deal with such a person, remember that you are defending yourself and your boundaries. Do not let that person make you feel absurd. As long as you have set a proper boundary, it does not matter how ridiculous it sounds; defend it. It also does not matter what the other person thinks about what you consider good and what you consider wrong.

Make sure that the person understands that whatever he/she is doing bothers you a lot, and if they keep doing it, you will walk away. Note again that the consequences you set have to be realized. If you tell a person that you will walk away from him/her for such behavior, do it. If you do not make your threats substantial, the person will start taking you as a joke and even overstep other boundaries. Do what you said you would do if the person crossed your boundaries. Failing to do so is a real deal-breaker.

Hijacking Matters

This is another technique used very often by both professional and non-professional manipulators. When using the hijacking method, the manipulator tries to distract you from the real matter at hand.

He/she takes the conversation in a different direction than that which you intended. For instance, if you are asking the person why he/she is late to class, instead of talking about the lateness, the person chooses to talk about the topic being covered in class, and how behind he/she is in the subject. Another good example is when you have set a date with someone, and he/she is really late yet does not call you to let you know what is delaying him/her. Then, once the person arrives, he/she does not bother to explain to you what happened. And when you question them and mention that you were really concerned, the person starts accusing you of being not understanding, saying that you did not even help them at that moment. He/she will even tell you how you are selfish.

Most manipulators will tell you a story that will deter you from asking for more explanations. For instance, they might explain how stressed they are at work and how things are hard financially. They will keep talking about different things and even get into a rant about it. It will gradually turn into a 'picking a fight' kind of conversation, where you will be accused of a lack of sympathy and understanding and how you always start a conflict.

After such a hijack, you will find yourself taking the defensive. You explain to the person that you totally underrated his/her position and that you empathize with them. In fact, you might start apologizing without even knowing why. At the end of the day, you will not get any explanations from the person, and what is even worse is that you will apologize for asking. All you wanted was to set a boundary, but now, it has become a battle that you no longer know what you wanted. You will find yourself soothing the manipulator and compromising their peace. In fact, you might never question him/her again because the poor thing is 'having a really hard time at work, in their personal lives, or at home.'

· · ·

If you wanted to set a boundary by telling a person that he/she should call you when he/she realizes he is getting late, make sure that you have your reasons ready. Manipulators are very good at taking the conversation to a different area.

When dealing with most manipulators, keep in mind that some of them are not conscious of their actions. In fact, most of us use the hijacking method when we are avoiding a conversation. A manipulator might not even be doing it on purpose — he/she could be trying to cover old scars or hide some weaknesses. If you notice this is happening, it is important first to take a break. For instance, if a person is hijacking your conversation, you need to get away from him/her and think.

At times, there is no point in trying to bring the conversation back to what it was before because this person will not listen at this moment. The best way is to step aside and let the person cool off, then engage later. However, there are times when you can tell the person straight in the face, that whatever he/she is talking about is miles away from the real conversation, then bring the conversation back.

Instead of trying to argue your way back to the original conversation, let it go and wait for the next opportunity. In this case, the next opportunity is as soon as the person has cooled down. Do not wait for too long before asking the person. Make sure that, by the evening of the following day, you have had the conversation and made your boundaries clear. Bring up the topic calmly, and if the person tries to suppress you again, say calmly, "I am not going to let you derail this conversation again because it is important to me." If they do not accept that, it is time to walk away.

Boundaries are really important, and if a person does not let you set

yours, he/she has no business being in your life. Get out of the relationships that make you feel intimidated when having conversations
about your boundaries. In fact, if you are in a relationship whenever
the partner blows things out of proportion every other time and
keeps derailing the conversations that are important to you, it is time
to reconsider the relationship.

Ultimatums

There are a lot of people who manipulate others using ultimatums.
This is more like giving conditions to the other person, such as,
"Either do this or else that happens," or, "You have to do this now,"
Basically, you do not get to decide if you want to do it or not. Ultimatums, as a manipulative tactic, are designed to make you jump into
decisions that are not in your best interest or you have not thought
about yet.

The best way to deal with ultimatums is to say no automatically. For
instance, if a person tells you that you have to present a report right
away, and you have not even prepared for it, just say no. You might
say yes, and maybe you make such a bad presentation because of the
limited preparation time, which might get you fired. Remember that
you already have your plans in place so, when a person needs you to
change your plans, he/she needs to ask you in advance and give you
some time to think about it. If he/she requires you to make up your
mind right away, then it is a no.

Most manipulative people will rush you into making decisions
without giving you enough time to consider all options. The reason
for this is that you do not get the time to assess all the requirements
and results. You must learn how to ask for time to think about something, even when it looks too good to leave out. The way a person
reacts when you ask for some time to think will tell you if it was a
genuine request or a manipulative tactic. A Person making a genuine
request will give you time to think.

Artificially Narrowing Options

This technique involves limiting your option so that you only settle for one, and, in most cases, that option favors the manipulator. A manipulator using this technique will give you only two viable options and use the ultimatum technique to squeeze you into choosing an option without careful consideration.

When you see this technique being put to play, stay objective and ask yourself, "Are these the only two options available? Is it possible to get better deals?" If you have some time and space to breathe, chances are, you will identify better options. But the manipulator does not want that, so he/she will keep knocking you out of time and giving you ultimatums. Most of the manipulators using this technique are aware of their actions.

A large number of salespeople and negotiators apply this method, more often than not. They are trying to fix you in a certain corner to suit them. The pressure and confusion will make you give in to demands and requests you would rarely take up. When you feel that someone is rushing you into making a decision, take a step back and ask for some time away from all the force. Remember that there are always other decisions, such as 'none of the above' or something completely different that is not so great for the manipulator but beneficial to you and probably does not cost as many resources as the other options.

Real negotiation and compromise do not result in one person winning and the other losing. Instead, it is about winning together and the option being beneficial to each other. Anyone who narrows your options down does now want a real win-win situation. Hopefully, you are not surrounded by manipulative people, but once in a while, these situations come up. Maybe there is that person who wants you to help them with money and is trying to show you that you must help them with that money, regardless of the results. In such a moment, it is best to walk away. Ask for time, and walk away even if they say no. This will buy you time to consider your options.

For instance, if a car dealer is pushing you into buying one car between the two units that he has already selected for you, even if there are others, take your time to think. These people will push you, and your brain will start going crazy with confusion. At that moment, stop and walk away. If the person is pushing you to take one of two decisions, chances are, none of the two decisions is really worthy, or they would not have to force you. Listen to your gut at the moment. If you are feeling pressured and stressed, it is time to leave.

The Principles

Manipulation is more common than you think, and persuasion is everywhere in your daily activities. In fact, if you think you have always been in control of your emotions, here is the disappointing news: you are not. We all want to believe that all the choices we make are personal. As we have mentioned earlier, studies show that the majority of us hate being told what to do, so we try as much as possible to make our own choices and follow them through. The need to be in control of personal choices has fooled most of us into thinking that no one can manipulate us. However, this is as false as it gets.

Every decision you have ever made was influenced by something, consciously or subconsciously. For instance, if you are a religious person, chances are, you picked that from your parents at a tender age, or you have learned about it in your adult life. If you like vegetables, there is a high likelihood that you have read or listened to many talks about the importance of these foods in our bodies. It does not sound like it, but persuasion exists everywhere. In fact, our brain is wired to look for something to guide it into making decisions. These guidelines are persuaders. Believe it or not, the decision-making process is tedious, and we unconsciously look for shortcuts, certain cues, and triggers to help us arrive at a conclusion.

. . .

Influence plays a great role in our lives, and since most companies understand this, they hire salespersons. Have you ever bought something from a salesperson because it sounded like a good deal, then you realize you do not really need the item when you get home? That is the power of persuasion, manipulation, and influence. The very techniques used by salespeople to get you to make that purchase are the same techniques used by scammers. In fact, bosses will use these same techniques to make you do a particular thing. Furthermore, they are the same techniques used by your boyfriend/girlfriend to get what they want. Here is the best part; you can use these techniques to manipulate the people around you and have your way.

If you are having dilemmas about manipulating people, you are not alone. A lot of people have conflicting feelings about these techniques because the term manipulation has been used to mean something negative for long. But think of it, if you have a close friend who is abusing drugs and people have tried to talk him/her out of it, to no avail, would you just leave things as they are? Or would you try to influence him/her? Of course, you will dedicate some time and effort into trying to influence that person to be better. Is that unethical? Definitely not — you are trying to help your friend, with a genuine heart. Manipulation techniques can be used to tune the thoughts of different people and make them give in to our requests. Whether you use manipulation for good or bad is up to you. And, if you choose to use manipulation techniques for the good of the world, then you will benefit more for a longer-term.

One thing you must take note of is one might want to ignore the facts about manipulation, but that will not make it go away. In fact, anyone who chooses to ignore these facts, and in this age and era, will suffer a lot and not only him/her but also his/her loved ones. Information is power, and how you choose to use it is up to you.

. . .

Persuasion is power. Imagine having the ability to make people do what you want without having to force them. Being able to use influence as a skill is actually a superpower. Luckily, research conducted over the years has revealed the various ways that people use to influence others. Persuasion and positive manipulation as superpowers are very much within reach of anyone interested. In this topic, we will explore the different principles of persuasion and the ways you can use them to your advantage.

Contrast Principle

This is a manipulation technique that has been used by many people over the years successfully. Chances are, you have been a victim of this. Basically, the contrast principle involves making something look more favorable than another by making a comparison. Have you ever walked into a store to buy, say, a stereo system, then the salesman showed you a really expensive one, to the extent you wanted to walk away?

This person might have mentioned all the good things about the system and all the reasons for selling it at that price, but you knew it was too expensive for you, so you started walking away. Then just at the final moment, the salesperson showed you a more affordable item, probably the same design with the same specifications, but for one reason or the other, it is better priced than the first one? And you could not help but think, "Wow, this is so much cheaper. I will buy it." In fact, you went ahead and bought it because, well, it is a *good* bargain.

Well, guess what, you did not really get a better bargain. The salesperson just used the contrast principle. He/she first showed you the expensive item first, then, just at the right time, he/she showed a cheaper item. And to you, that sounded like a good bargain. If you had been introduced to the cheaper item first, with nothing to compare it with, would you still have gotten it? Probably not. But in this case, it feels like a win. Technically, this is the same technique used by supermarkets and most stores to make you buy an item. You will see a tag showing a before and an after price. The 'before' price will be higher than the 'now' price. Remember that your mind is wired to look for cues, so, these prices will be the trigger. First, your mind will register the huge price, then compare it with the lower price, and boom, you have the bargain to rush to.

Human beings have a problem of recognizing and understanding the objective value of an item. Therefore, they need something to compare it to. You will only call someone 'short' because you can see the people around him/her are 'taller.' Something only appears expensive if there are similar items going for a lower price. If, you only have one item sold at a particular price, and there were no competing items, chances are, we could buy them without much fuss.

So, if you have a business and want to make the customer buy more items on account of the contrast principle, give more offers. Multiple offers priced differently will give the customer more points of comparison and valuation. If you want to protect yourself and your loved ones from this technique, make sure that you view the object of manipulation. For instance, if a salesperson shows you an expensive item then tell you that it is being sold at a lower price for some reason, view it in light of the offer price only and ignore the original price. Is the item something you would want to buy at the 'after price' or not?

Reciprocity

Reciprocity involves giving something to someone in an attempt to repay them for a favor they did. Have you ever done someone a favor simply because they had done you one earlier? That is the reciprocation tendency. Basically, we as human beings, are social animals and will do anything to fit in. People do not want to seem like they are not contributing to society. Therefore, the majority of us will not allow others to do favors without reciprocating. If someone does something for us, we feel obligated to pay them back. Most companies and organizations have discovered this weakness in the human brain and are using it to attract customers. Salespersons know that giving a gift will trigger reciprocation, probably making the person to purchase an item.

Interesting fact, one does not need to do a big favor in order to trigger these feeling of "giving in return." A study conducted in restaurants revealed the strength of reciprocation, and it does not really come with the size of the favor but the strategy behind it. The study revealed that when a waiter gave the customer a sweet alongside the bill, he/she was more likely to tip than when given the bill only. Again, when the customer got two sweets alongside the bill, he/she gave a higher tip compared to the two previous scenarios. Finally, when the waiter gave the customer one sweet alongside the bill then went away for a while and came back with two more sweets and said, "This is for you for being such a lovely person," the tip was even higher. It was not really the size of the gift but the impact on the emotions. You feel special. Thus, you feel like giving something back in an attempt to make the person experience what you have.

This idea of reciprocation is what leads most companies into giving free keychains, caps, shirts, and samples. They know that even if you do not buy the product right away, there is a likelihood of making the purchase in the future. You will remember that nice feeling.

How can you protect yourself from this form of manipulation? First, you may turn down the offer of the gift politely. You can simply tell the salesperson, "Thank you, but I do not need that right now," or "Sorry, I am in a hurry, maybe next time." There are cases where you cannot avoid taking the gift. Then it is only safe for you to think of the gift as an ordinary thing. Do not make a purchase just because you were given a gift. Stay objective when shopping for an item. Think:

"Would I buy this without the gift?" Regardless of the situation, do not be rude to the people trying to sell to you. Be kind and encouraging, but do not fall into the trap.

Concession

The concession is more like the door in the face technique where you start by asking for a big favor, and when the person says "no," you mention the smaller request. Remember the example earlier about a kid asking for a $50 from the parents? In this case, when a parent says no, and the kid says, "Can I at least have 10?" chances are, the parent will say yes. Robert Cialdini talks about a little girl who manipulated him into buying a chocolate bar successfully. First, this girl approached Robert and asked him to buy a box of cookies which he turned down. Then the girl asked him to at least buy a box of chocolate, and he said yes. He only realized that the girl had successfully manipulated him after the purchase.

In simple terms, you have to make the first request sound a bit unachievable but not too outrageous, and once the person says no, make it sound simpler. This change makes you seem like a reasonable person. Most of the time, people agree to a smaller request than big ones.

Commitment and Consistency

Studies have revealed that people like to appear consistent. That is, their word is in line with their actions. We tend to like people who keep their word and associate such with discipline and achievement. So if a person says that he/she will do a particular thing at a certain time, more so in the presence of people, chances are, he/she will try to stay consistent by doing it.

In particular, researchers did research to understand the power of commitment and consistency. First, they went to one neighborhood and asked the people there to put small signs of 'drive safely' on the window. They agreed to it. After some time, they went to the same neighborhood and asked the people to put up another sign that was really ugly, and they agreed. However, when they went to a different neighborhood and asked the members to put up the bigger ugly sign, the people there refused. Since the first neighborhood had already agreed to put up a small sign, they agreed to add the second sign, simply because of consistency. They did not want to seem like rebels.

The commitment or consistency principle explains that human beings have a deep need to be consistent/stable and also to be seen as such. So, every time a person commits to something publicly, he/she will try his/her best to meet it. So making a person commit to something will somehow force him/her to stay consistent. The consistency principle is based on the strength of public, voluntary, and active commitments that make people commit to their word.

The first step to making someone commit and hold his/her end of the bargain is by making it active. By 'active,' we mean something that is said or written to the other, something evident. Having a person say he/she will do something is a start, but making that person follow through requires an activation step.

The next step involves making it public. When there are witnesses in a commitment, it increases accountability. The person who made the promise will have to keep his/her word because more people are watching. That is why most commitments, such as marriage, require a witness. Most people avoid going back on their word when there are many others involved.

Finally, to have someone make a promise and keep it, he/she should do it voluntarily.

Basically, we do not like to do things that have been forced upon us by others. Researchers have found that people are more likely to hold a bargain if they think they made a choice. If you force anyone to do something they do not like, there are high chances that he/she will not offer the best service. So the only way to make people be consistent is by making them feel that they have made the decisions themselves.

Social Proof

This principle is based on the fact that we are social creatures. We do not want to look too defiant. We tend to follow what is normal. Have you ever been in a unique situation where you did not really know how to react, therefore you looked at how others were reacting? That was you, looking for a guideline on what is normal. It is something we do often and unconsciously.

It is human nature to rely on cues from other people. Our minds are unknowingly paying attention to what others are doing and copying them. So, whenever we find ourselves in a situation where we do not know what to do, our nature forces us to look at other people, especially those we believe are similar to us. That is termed as social proof. It is the reason that you are more likely to go to an eatery that is always full. It is also the reason you are likely to work a little late because your co-workers are doing the same.

Technically, if something is being done by a 'large' number of people, it must be right or at least acceptable. Having a person take particular action at the right time makes all the difference.

Have you ever wondered why some advertisements use testimonials to advertise their products? Have you noticed that we enjoy what other people seem to enjoy and dismiss what other people are dismissing? That is social proof. People follow what the majority seem to be doing because 'everyone is doing it; therefore, it cannot be wrong.' If a good number of people recommend a particular item to you, chances are, you will buy it, too, even if you doubt the testimonies.

. . .

The social proof principle can be used to get an advantage. For instance, if you are going to give a talk somewhere, instead of introducing yourself, you let someone else introduce you. When you introduce yourself and talk about your achievement before the talk, some people will feel like you are bragging. However, if someone else mentions how you been an achiever in life and state the specific accomplishment, the audience will take note of what you have to say. That establishes social proof. It is important to avoid establishing social proof for yourself because you will come off as a show-off.

Liking

You have heard people complaining that the hot girl or the handsome man got a promotion while everyone else was just overlooked. Why is it that charming people are more likely to reach their goals than others? The secret is liking. Good looks have an effect on people; we often associate them with good things. And we are easily persuaded by things we like. We like different people for different reasons, sometimes, even the simplest ones. It is possible to like someone just because he/she comes from your hometown, or maybe you have things in common. You could even like a person just because you like him/her — no solid reasons, just vibes. It has been found that we are more attentive to people we like, what they say, and how they affect us.

The feeling of liking someone is very complex; therefore, it can make one do things he/she would not ordinarily do. So, how can you avoid the effects of these principles? Be rational and think, "Would I listen to this person and what he/she is saying if I did not like them? Is their request reasonable? Or are you just falling for the charm? To use this technique to your advantage, always look your best, make yourself likable, and have the appeal. Stay charming. Smile a lot and become a good conversationalist.

Another way of making people like you is through finding common ground with them. Once you meet a person, establish the things you have in common and use them to connect. These commonalities could be hobbies, living or hailing from the same area, having studied the same course, and others. Be observant of people; this will help you pick cues from them that will lead to a common ground.

Finally, the easiest way of making people develop a liking for you is through genuine praise. Being charming and paying compliments to people will go a long way into building a rapport with them. Beware, though, not to go overboard with the compliments and the charming façade. It will raise the alarm. The key is to stay genuine; avoid manufacturing compliments to the point where it is evident that you are buttering up the person.

Authority

Authority enables one to command attention, directly or indirectly. Interestingly, people do not need to know what you have achieved in order to associate you with authority. So long as you look like it, you have it. Fake confidence if you must, and people will actually pay attention.

Authority will help you to make people do what you want. However, there is a way to establish authority. If people know that you have command/expertise in a certain area, they will come to you for help. Why? Because they know that you will offer them a shortcut in the field and a good decision.

Titles, such as Dr. and uniforms, such as police uniforms, can bring the air of authority. And an average person will follow that authority without question. That is why most advertisements use certain figures and images in front of their campaigns.

You see, if a child walks up to you and starts explaining to you the meaning of life, chances are, you will ignore whatever he/she has to say, even if it is completely profound. However, if a person who looks great in a well-fitted designer suit and amazing shoe walks up to you and repeats the same words said by the child, you will listen. In fact, you will hang onto every word like it is the most insightful thing discovered in life. This is because the physical appearance of the older person can be associated with authority, unlike the small child. Now, this is a major problem in life.

We often judge by what we see. And that is why we keep choosing the wrong leaders; we often listen to unreal promises and believe them just because they are said by a successful politician while ignoring real facts said by ordinary people.

Basically, we look for people who look like they mean what they say. How can that small child who was explaining to you about life even know what he/she is talking about? The older man must have lived and experienced some things in life; therefore, he knows what he is talking about.

The challenge only arises when the authority is just perceived, meaning, it is unreal. Most of us will do something simply because the person asking seems to have authority. You could stop your car simply because a policeman asked you to, even if you are not sure if he/she is a real cop. Just because he/she looks like a police officer, with authority to stop you, that assumption makes you stop. As long as the right amount of confidence is applied, anyone can create the illusion of authority. To use this principle to your advantage, make sure that you have the right amount of confidence, dress right, and display your achievements.

You might miss this opportunity of authority if you just assume that people will detect it automatically. There are steps you have to take to establish such authority. The first and easiest step is to make your achievement visible. For instance, if you have a diploma in psychology, display it in your office and house. Any relevant award should be made public. However, do not overdo this because it might look like bragging. Another way of establishing authority is by sharing your qualifications during conversations. Remember that no one can detect your expertise without some information. Make sure you have passed the right information to your target.

How can you protect yourself from falling for this principle of manipulation? Always ask yourself these: "would I do this if the request was not from an authoritative person?" "Is this request reasonable?" "Can I ask for such a favor?"

Scarcity

We, as human beings, are fairly motivated by the thought of getting and achieving, and that is why we look for more — higher education, better cars and houses, and better lifestyles. However, you might be surprised to learn that we are also afraid of losing. In fact, we are more afraid of losing than we are of gaining. And that is why we rush for opportunities-so that we do not lose them.

Have you noticed that almost all the stores have a sale offer? Or every once in a while, companies put things on offer and give them a time limit? For instance, "buy this jacket, the price is down by $50 for the next 24 hours. Get it now." Some of the products sold online have a countdown, showing that it is only available for a while. That limitation makes it exciting; we have to get the bird before it flies away.

The basic supply and demand principle is used to manipulate people. To be precise, what is scarce is highly valued. The rarer a commodity is, the higher the demand. Think of valuables such as gold and diamond. They are so expensive simply because they are not easy to find.

Creating a scarcity will make people want to get whatever the item is. There are several ways of creating scarcity — limit the supply, make limited-time offers, and create one-time opportunities. These offers create an immediate sense of scarcity.

Again, the way you present these offers matters as it will affect the impact. When making this offer, concentrate on telling the target group what they will miss if they fail to take the offer. The feeling of loss has a greater impact on the mind than the gain.

Another way of creating a feeling of scarcity is through the exclusivity approach. This involves sharing information only to a particular group of people while leaving out others. Exclusivity approach makes the target feel special, therefore more likely to take the offer. The people accessing this information fell like they are favored or valued more than others.

62

To detect and avoid this form of manipulation, ask yourself, "Would I get that product if it was not on offer?" Do you really need it, or are you just hurrying to catch the opportunity? Think for a few minutes and make a sober decision.

HOW TO READ ANYONE

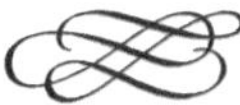

An ability to read a person would protect us from a lot of things, such as unnecessary guesswork or the anxiety over the feedback we might get from clients. In fact, this ability would help you excel in a lot of areas in your life.

According to research done over the years on communication, we only pass 7 percent of information through words. The remaining 93 percent is information passed through body language and voice tone. It is, therefore, very important to be able to read the body language of a person as much as listening to what they are saying. Facial expression and the way one holds his/her eyes will tell you a lot about what the person is thinking and his/her personality. In this case, we will discuss how you can quickly assess the inner character of a person and understand who they are.

The art of reading a person involves not only understanding what they say but also who they really are. Most of the successful psychiatrists and leaders use their mind-reading skills to ignite the super sense of understanding different personalities. Reading a person requires you to be able to interpret both verbal and non-verbal cues. That is, the ability to see past mask dawned by an individual. In most cases, logic will not tell the real story of a person. You have to involve other vital forms of information to know the person truly. Basically, people have things they want to hide, and as such, they will avoid sharing them. With the right skills for reading people, you will be able to see what is right in front of you and what is not. That is why it is important for you to learn how to interpret the non-verbal, intuitive cues given by people.

For you to read people correctly, you must be willing to give up any misgivings, emotional baggage, or wrongful assumptions that might limit your ability to understand a person. This may involve ego clashes and resentments. For example, the assumption that all men should not feel or display any emotions might hinder you from realizing that a man is as human as any other person.

The only way to understand anyone is to remain objective and get information neutrally without altering or destroying it. For instance, do not assume that all cats are lactose tolerant just because you were taught that all cats drink milk. You will be surprised to learn that some cats fall sick when they take milk. Yes, it is a fact; there are lactose-intolerant cats. But that is not the rule, either.

Whoever you are reading, be it your co-worker, partner, or your boss, to understand people, you have to surrender any biases you have already set. Any person who knows how to read another person well has already learned how to use what is referred to as super sense. It is the ability to look further than just the surface.

Techniques You Can Use to Read Someone

There are several techniques you can use to read someone, depending on the situation.

The Question Technique

The question technique involves asking the subject for an opinion about something. It is an extremely simple yet effective way of learning about a person. This will not only give you an insight into the person but also yourself. The best thing to ask about is another person. For instance, you can ask a co-worker about another colleague.

A study conducted in one university by psychologists revealed that most people would judge others by how they perceive themselves. The study was conducted on students who were asked to rate the personalities of their acquaintances.

Basically, people will define others by their own personality. Have you ever heard of the saying, "it says more about them than it says about me," especially when a person is saying mean things about the other? It is true that people will judge you by how they feel about themselves. If a person classifies others as selfish and not understanding, chances are, he/she is selfish and lacking understanding. If someone calls other people happy and fun, there is a high likelihood that he/she is also happy.

After a number of students had classified their acquaintances, the psychologists found that the students were more likely to display the personality traits they used to rate others. The way we classify people reflects the way we feel. The students who rated others as light-hearted and kind were more likely to display kindness and light-heartedness. Those who rated others as being manipulative and negative had their own psychological issues.

In conclusion, the psychologists stated that the tendency to view people in negative light indicates a greater possibility of having personality disorders, so if you want to know who a person is and what he/she might be going through, ask them what they think of others. Better still, pay attention to how a person treats and talks about those around him/her, for instance, close friends, relatives, or loved ones.

Intuition

Learning how to listen to your intuition takes time. However, once a person has mastered how to listen to his/her intuition and trust it, he/she can read people correctly most of the time. Intuition tells you more about a person than both words and body language. In fact, some psychologists say it is the surest way of learning about a person. Basically, intuition is what your guts tell you as soon as you encounter a person. It has nothing to do with your analysis or thoughts. Therefore, there are high chances of being right.

Intuition can also be defined as the nonverbal information you perceive without logic. Some say that intuition is the information that you *feel*. When you read a person or situation with intuition, it allows you to gather more information and see deeper than the obvious. You get a glimpse of the true personality of that person.

The ability to use intuition correctly comes with time. The first way of practicing this skill is to honor your gut feelings.

1. **Listen carefully.** You have to honor your gut feelings. Listen to your guts more so when you meet a person for the first time. Pay attention to that visceral reaction that occurs within you before your brain and logic kick in. Technically, we are wired to survive. So, our bodies have a way of reading a situation and responding to it long before you can even think. It is the same sense that allows you to fight or flight in case of danger, long before your brain can process all the facts. The feeling you get after meeting a person for the first time relays to you some information – are you at ease or not? Gut feeling is a very primal feeling and will occur very quickly. If you are not on the lookout, you might miss the signs or simply ignore that intuition. Using intuition, you can decide whether to trust a person or not.

Think of your intuition as an internal truth meter that helps you to determine what another person is like.

1. **Feel the goosebumps.** Goosebumps are the intuitive tingles that inform you when a person is inspiring or moving you. You will also feel goosebumps if someone says something that tags at your chord of character. If you pay close attention to the goosebumps occurring on your skin, it might be a good source of information on the kind of a person you are dealing with.

1. **Pay attention to flashes of insight.** Your body knows more than you can imagine. There is a saying that goes, "your heart knows reasons which your mind is not aware of and vice versa." When having a conversation with someone, there are things you will notice, which will show you the true character of the person. However, some of these signs are so subtle that we ignore them. Most of the time, we are so focused on the next thought that we lose the current moment and facts. There is always that *ah-ha* moment where you feel that you have a glimpse of the real character of a person. Normally, that is intuition at work, and such flashes get lost in the chatter. Now that you know about it, pay attention.

2. **Watch the eyes.** You have heard the saying that the eyes are the window to the soul. It is quite true. You can tell a lot about a person by the way they move their eyes. Majority of us have our personalities written in our eyes. Like the body itself, the eyes can transmit different energies, for instance, anger, meanness, tranquility, and sexiness. If you take your time to look at someone's eyes, it will be easy to tell if the person is angry, bitter, lost, insecure, happy, kind, or guarded. Though there are people who have eyes that differ from the content of their personality, most of them have things in common. When reading the personality of a

person by watching the eyes, you will be using intuition once again.

3. **Listen to the voice tone and laugh.** Understanding what different tones in the voice of a person represent will enable you to understand him/her. The volume of the voice and the kind of laugh will tell you a lot about a person and the situation. Sound frequencies create vibrations. You should notice how the voice tone of a person affects you. Does the tone make you comfortable or throw you off balance? Is it soothing, whiny, snippy, or hash? Is their laughter genuine or mischievous? This information will guide you on whether to continue with the conversation or change it.

4. **Look out for intuitive empathy.** There are times when you will feel the physical and emotional symptoms of a person. This normally arises from empathy. The feeling and emotions you detect in the other person will give you a glimpse of their personality or at least what they are going through.

Sense Motional Emotional Energy

Emotion is a stunning expression of our energy. We have the special ability to register some of the vibrations given off by a person. We gather most of these vibes through intuition. You will be able to detect when a person likes to be around you. You will also sense those who do not like your presence. By listening to the emotional vibrations, you will be able to tell who is adding to or draining your positive energy. These subtle feelings should be noted.

Below are some more clues on how you can read and gauge a person.

How can you tell if a person is an introvert or an extrovert?

The easiest way to tell if a person is introverted or extroverted is by watching the way a person responds to a question.

Basically, if you ask someone a question and he/she responds immediately as if thinking out loud, the chances are, that is an extrovert, or he/she has an extroverted personality. Many extroverts are very outspoken and do not hesitate to share their thoughts. So, when a question arises, they respond very fast.

For people with introverted personalities, it is quite the opposite. If you ask them a question, they take some seconds before answering; it is like they are weighing their words. By understanding the different personalities in people, you can improve your reactions to situations. For instance, you will understand that a delay in responding does not always indicate a lack of knowledge. In some cases, delayed responses represent introverted personalities. If you have an extroverted personality and you are talking to an introvert, ensure that you give him/her enough time to respond.

It takes time and effort to practice reading people, but the ability to pick different subtle cues that most people would miss gives you an upper hand.

Basic psychology tells us that we tend to move away from uncomfortable situations as we grow up. If, for example, you had a tough childhood where the other kids were always picking on you, chances are, you will do everything in your power to avoid such situations as you get older.

Imagine a child who came from a very poor background and did not have nice clothes or the best meals. When this child went to school, he/she saw other kids with nice clothes, perfect shoes, good meals, and other nicer things. This created a desire in him/her — to have nice things, too. As this child gets older, he/she will look for the nice things, unknowingly.

· · ·

If a person was not picked for basketball at gym class or was hardly the best in class, and maybe other kids and even teachers picked on him/her, he/she learns how to associate certain things and situations with failure. Therefore, he/she would look for a way to avoid them. You will find that such people will want only those things that make them appear stronger, for instance, the getting to a bigger position, wearing the best clothes and shoes, buying the best car that money can buy, and going to the gym in order to get bigger muscles.

Once we understand that some people are doing things in order to move away from certain forms of pain in their past life, it becomes easier to tolerate and even guide them. This understanding can also help us to understand why we do the things we do. Such knowledge will also enable us to decide if we want a particular person in our lives or not.

The Shoes

This is an insanely powerful trick, and even though it will sound absurd, it works. Did you know that you can tell a lot about a person by looking at their shoes? Now you know. Someone can easily tell about 90 percent of your personality from your shoes. According to research conducted in the University of Kansas, the psychologists found that it is possible to tell the personality of a person from their shoes. Shoes can tell a person about your political affiliation, emotional state, income, age, gender, and life experiences.

In the study, some students were asked to look at the pictures of 208 different pairs of shoes and describe the personality of the wearer without seeing him/her. The owners of the shoes had filled out a personality test which was used to compare the predictions of the students with the reality. The results were quite unexpected.

The study found that flashy and colorful shoes belonged to extroverts, while expensive shoes were from high-income earners. The shoes that were not very new but looked spotless were from people with a conscientious personality. Other shoes that looked practical were from people with an agreeable personality, while ankle boots were owned by those with an aggressive personality. People with unkempt shoes have a calm personality, while those extremely well-kept, brand-new shoes belonged to people who have attachment anxiety issues. In fact, these extremely well-kept shoes indicate that the person might be having problems with his/her relationships.

Here is the most interesting finding; people with less expensive shoes are liberal thinkers, not just low-income earners. This next point should not come to you as a surprise either. Boring shoes indicate that the wearer does not care what other people think of them and are also people who have a hard time forming relationships.

Although these observations are not the rule of law, most of them are true. So, from now on, remember that your shoes tell a lot about you. Which statement do you want to make?

Social Media

Is it possible to tell the personality of a person from their social media platforms? Yes, it is. You can tell a lot about a person from their profile picture and the messages they share. The AAI digital library conducted and published a study that states that it is possible to discover the personality of a person by looking at their profile picture. This study found that most people who have simple photos with less color and displayed blank expressions with partially hidden features scored higher for neuroticism. In simple terms, people with neurotic personalities are more likely to be negative about the future. They tend to judge other people negatively and have excess feelings of anxiety. They get feelings of anger, guilt, and envy much more than normal people.

· · ·

The study also revealed that people with extroverted personalities normally have other people in the picture. They also have photos with more color and very wide smiles. The best-looking profile pictures belonged to people who were most open to new experiences. Such people have photos with higher contracts, and the images are sharper. The face of the person takes up more of the picture.

Surprisingly, the study revealed that people with bad profile photos were likely to be highly agreeable. Such people will post bad pictures of themselves, but they are normally bright and lively. They are also always smiling.

The ability to read the true personality of a person or the inner character gives you an extreme advantage over other people who lack the same skill. Reading people is an ability you can use to improve every area of your life. You might not be very good at first, but with enough practice, you will become better. Practice this skill around other people and pay attention to what is happening in your own life.

Gradually, you will be able to understand different personalities quickly and effectively. And depending on the situation, the ability to read people could earn you a lot at the poker table. It might even save your life.

Other Effective Tools for Reading People

How to use the skills of reading others effectively and combine them with persuasion skills? Many people think that the skill of reading people can only be acquired in a psychology class. Well, that is not entirely true. In fact, being in a psychology class does not guarantee the ability to manipulate, persuade, influence, or read others. Such skills are the choice of anyone who wants to be influential, powerful, and skilled. It is very hard to read, manipulate, or influence a person who knows how to read people. That is why you need to learn the different ways of reading people and what their intentions are before they even tell you.

The ability to read others is advantageous because it enables one to see through people's intentions. If you want to get significant power, it is important to understand how you can read people and apply the information you gather. Making a deal with the wrong person will most probably cost you an opportunity. The only way to know if the deal is favorable or unfavorable to you is by reading the other person. You can hardly get all the information through listening to their words.

Reading a person is not as simple as looking at their body posture, listening to their tone of voice, or watching how they hold their eyes. No, it runs much deeper than that. Below are some of the techniques you need to learn in order to read, manipulate, and persuade people successfully.

1. Master subtextual communication

To have an effective level of reading people, your ability to observe the unseen must be high. Your perception of indirect communication must be sharp. You must understand the actions and words of people on multiple levels. Remember that communication has different levels. It is very important to analyze what is said, what is truly said, what is actually meant that could be implied.

To practice this skill, try and read the people around you and analyze what they say, mean, and imply. They can be your friends, family, or neighbors. The most important thing is to observe them and take note of their words and actions. Are they aligned, or does the person say one thing and mean another? What are the values of different people around you, and what drives them? Such information can help you to predict the future moves of a person.

Poker players study their opponent's moves and bluffs so that they can predict how others think. With enough time and practice, these poker players are able to predict the thoughts of the person correctly. Write down what your *target* person values and analyze ways you can use it for your benefit. For instance, a kind person may value integrity and honesty while hating manipulators.

Once you understand that, it is easy to persuade and even manipulate such a person. A loud person who talks a lot may value one who listens to him/her patiently. In fact, such a person may hate other extroverts who will talk more. Once you understand what makes a person tick, you can manipulate him/her. On the other hand, when you understand the things that are valuable to you, it becomes easy to tell when and how another person can manipulate you.

The average person is normally unaware of the potential and dynamics hidden in the environment. And that is why the power-hungry people appreciate the sleeping society. Heightened powers of observation can be seen as threatening to the person who uses manipulation to get his/her way.

Although having a strong ability to make an observation is harmless, some people will see it as a threat. They will feel that you are hindering their personal interests. Others will find it hard to trust you because of the inherent paranoia that your abilities will expose them. This is why the ability to appear unintelligent is useful in some situations. Looking unknowledgeable is a necessary and most effective form of concealment.

1. Think logically

Most of us use emotions to analyze situations and make decisions. Now, to be able to read people correctly, you need to learn how to use logic and not emotion. People who are good at reading others possess a high degree of self-control, especially when it comes to emotions. They do not get easily moved by situations. Instead, they are open-minded and prefer to work with facts, reasoning, and logic. Such people are close-minded to opinions and are not easily manipulated even by charm. Regardless of what others say, people who use logic will still look for the facts and analyze the data without bias.

To practice using logic, instead of lashing out at someone when you are angry, take some time to calm yourself down and get away from acting impulsively. At first, it might be hard to change from using emotions to using logic, but with practice, you will find it easier to stay calm and think rationally regardless of the situation. Look for ways to master your emotions. In most cases, emotional reasoning leads to incorrect deductions because of poor judgment and loss of self-control.

1. Develop wit

Human beings test each other in order to classify one another. This classification tells a person how he/she can deal with you. If you have a strong wit, people will back down, but if you show signs of weakness and insecurity, they will manipulate you. For example, a girl can test your confidence and insecurities by making a remark about your weaknesses. She could also test you by asking a question that puts you in a bad light. Most politicians and celebrities get tested by their colleagues by putting them in a bad light. They will make negative comments and wait for the person to reply. Normally, this is a trap.

· · ·

If your wit is not developed well, these daily attacks can get to you and make you react badly. Consequently, you will look bad. For instance, in the earlier mentioned case scenario where the girl makes selfish remarks, you might be tempted to retaliate with a negative comment, then people will perceive you as a bad person. This will lower your value.

However, if you have a well-developed wit, it will be easy to deflect any negative energy back to the sender. In fact, with the right wit, you can easily use the things meant to bring you down to your advantage and boost your social value. To improve and develop your wit, engage more with people and get into light-hearted banters with colleagues and friends. In developing wit, the experience is very important.

1. Emotional intelligence

Emotional intelligence is the ability to read the emotions of other people and control yours. This kind of intelligence is rare and very valuable. Empathy is also very important, and it plays a huge role in how we understand situations and relate to other people. It enables us to put ourselves in the shoes of others and somehow feel what they are going through. To develop emotional intelligence, you will need to feel and understand what other people feel and how they think. Empathy will enable you to become that person in a split second and understand the reasons behind their views. Those with low empathy cannot really understand others, and consequently, they lack emotional intelligence. All they know and relate to is their own emotions and point of view.

When you are able to understand where another person is coming from in terms of thought, it gives you a special power. You will know exactly how that person feels and things and possibly predict their next action correctly. It is very hard to truly understand a person and still stay in conflict with him/her. Getting an insight into the things going on in a person enables you to embrace them and make a decision on whether you want them closer to you or far.

Emotional intelligence enables you to stay in control. This intelligence allows you to understand and embrace different feelings. Hence, you will be able to control and even hide your real feelings, depending on the situation. You will also be able to influence the emotions of other people.

1. Cold reading

This technique involves gathering cold, hard facts on a person and rationalizing them. Cold reading is a very important aspect when you want to read people correctly. If you have the right facts, the chances of coming up with a correct theory about the person are high.

To practice this technique, gather data about the people around you, come up with a theory, and ask them if the conclusions you have arrived at are true. It is okay to be wrong at first. We learn through mistakes. With the right amount of practice, you will be able to read people correctly.

It is very important to gather enough data first before coming up with a conclusion because once you have the theory without enough data, your deductions and conclusion will be unreliable. For instance, you can see a person wearing expensive shoes and think or rationalize that he/she is a high-income earner. However, that person might have gotten it as a gift or, maybe he/she saved money for a whole year in order to buy it. Make sure that you have the right amount of information to make the right deduction. The ability to cold read a person correctly without even having to psychoanalyze them gives you a huge advantage over those who lack the skill of analyzing nonverbal cues.

1. Superficial charm

Reading people correctly requires you to have superficial charm. This is the ability to make a person relate to you and, consequently, give you information about them. Every interaction you have with others should have meaning. While chatting, you should be warming people up and gathering the information that helps you understand their nature.

When you understand another person, it becomes easier to calibrate your character to be similar to theirs, thus successfully socializing to people in different fields comfortably. Charm is a very important asset for comfort. And comfort is essential in building trust. Before a person trusts you, he/she has to feel comfortable around you. Without trust, your options for manipulating and reading people are limited. To practice superficial chart, start by mirroring the behavior of the people you meet. If a person is confident, you, too, should present a confident face, just within their range. Remember that the fastest way to make someone trusts you is by mirroring their behavior so that they can see similarities between you and them.

People tend to love themselves and cherish their own beliefs. If you show interest in them and whatever they believe in, they will love you for that, become comfortable with you, and develop trust. The next possible thing is that these people will open up to you. If you behave like a teenager around older people, they will consider you slightly immature, and they will not open up. Similarly, if you behave like a tough parent in the presence of teenagers, they will not open up. It is very important to adjust your behavior according to the people around you and the situation. Once you have trust from the group, you can influence, manipulate, and even persuade them as you please.

These techniques will help you to read people correctly, manipulate, persuade, and even influence crowds. Follow the instructions and practice them often.

AFTERWORD

There we have it — the manipulation, persuasion, and communication techniques that you can use to improve your life. The tips mentioned and explained here can be used to change our position. Use them proudly and enjoy the changes you will experience gradually. With time and practice, you will be able to tell the difference between genuine requests and manipulation techniques. In fact, you will be so good at reading people that making them do what you want and escaping their traps become easy tasks. Better still, you will be in an advantageous position to understand and influence a wide variety of people.

Remember that you have gotten an insight into a world unknown to many. For instance, a large number of people know that shoes tell a lot about a person. However, not many people can interpret the message right. Use this information to your advantage. Many people use emotions instead of logic to make decisions and act. You, on the other hand, are now informed about emotional intelligence and the role it plays in your life. Practice it and make your life better. I intentionally used a simple language in this book to make sure that everyone understands the power and ways of manipulation. It is now time to apply what you have learned and change your world.